THE SYNCHRONICITY JOURNAL

YOUR PERSONAL RECORD
of Signs Big and Small

TRISH Mac**GREGOR** AND **ROB M**ac**GREGOR**

AVON, MASSACHUSETTS

Published by
Adams Media, a division of F+W Media, Inc.
57 Littlefield Street, Avon, MA 02322. U.S.A.
www.adamsmedia.com

Contains material adapted and abridged from *The 7 Secrets of Synchronicity*
by Trish MacGregor and Rob MacGregor, copyright © 2010 by Trish MacGregor
and Rob MacGregor, ISBN 10: 1-4405-0391-5, ISBN 13: 978-1-4405-0391-7.

ISBN 10: 1-4405-2673-7
ISBN 13: 978-1-4405-2673-2

Printed in the United States of America.

10 9 8 7 6 5 4 3 2 1

leaves © istockphoto/borchee; branch © istockphoto/bibikoff;
dandelion © istockphoto/iSci; butterfly © istockphoto/cyfrogclone

*This book is available at quantity discounts for bulk purchases.
For information, please call 1-800-289-0963.*

CONTENTS

INTRODUCTION

When events in your life slide together like pieces in a cosmic puzzle, you might think of it as luck or coincidence. But synchronicity is much more than that. Carl Jung, who coined the term, defined synchronicity as the coming together of inner and outer events in a way that is meaningful to the observer and can't be explained by cause and effect. In other words, meaningful coincidence.

Synchronicity could very well prove to be the language of the cosmos, the way the universe communicates with you. Once you become aware of it, the experiences tend to proliferate. You begin to notice meaningful patterns in your life. You realize you're opening yourself to new information, new possibilities, new beliefs. All that's required is that you pay attention, be aware of so-called coincidences, and "capture" them. If you don't, they'll slip away like fragments of a dream after you awaken.

The very act of recognizing and recording synchronicities allows you to attune to the beat of the cosmos. Even though the meaning of a given synchronicity may not be immediately apparent, keep in mind that events happen for a reason.

In January of 2011, we went to the Florida Keys to help our daughter get situated for a month-long internship at a dolphin facility. Her college requires students to participate in an independent study project of their choice at least three times during their four years of study. One year, she went to Ecuador to volunteer at a wildlife rescue center in the jungle. For her senior year, it's dolphins in the Keys, at a facility where Megan swam with dolphins when she was much younger. We took two cars, with Rob and Trish ahead of Megan and her boyfriend.

There's an exhilarating moment in this drive when you reach the end of the Florida turnpike, the road narrows to two lanes, and suddenly you're on U.S. 1, which extends from Key West to Maine, and a sign announces that you're entering the Florida Keys.

It's called the Florida Keys Scenic Highway. It's 106.5 miles long and takes about four hours to drive from one end to the other. The Keys are an archipelago of 1,700 islands connected by bridges. The seven-mile bridge, the longest one, is an engineering marvel, with the Atlantic stretching out on one side of the road and the Gulf of Mexico stretching out on the other. The shades of blue and green are pure and clear; the air smells of salt, sand, and sun; and the sky looms from horizon to horizon. The beauty blows your mind and heart wide open; you kick off your shoes, lower your windows, and the breeze blows through the car. Suddenly you know that anything is possible. *You expect the miraculous.*

That mindset undoubtedly helped to attract a synchronicity just as we approached Key Largo. There, on the Gulf side of the highway, close to shore, a pod of five dolphins surfaced, their bodies shimmering in the cool light. We've been to the Keys dozens of times and have *never* seen a pod of dolphins during this drive. The synchronicity of it, the fact that we were down here because of Megan's internship at a dolphin research center, struck us as a favorable sign for her month's stay. We later realized the *five* was also significant: Megan's full name adds up to a five. In numerology, five is about travel and variety, seeking new horizons, getting a new point of view.

As it turned out, her internship was a resounding success and she has applied for a job there when she graduates.

These synchronicities illustrate the underlying unity of life, what physicist David Bohm called the implicate or enfolded order from which all life springs. When you become aware of synchronicity, the patterns in your life become more obvious. You move ahead smoothly. Even when you face setbacks and are unable to see how events are working in your favor, you may later realize that what happened was for the best. So in spite of your misgivings, it's vital to trust that the universe is on your side, working for you rather than against you.

Once you realize there's more to life than what you experience in your everyday world, you're on your way. It's easier to step back from your busy life with its multitasking and to-do lists and take time to contemplate the big picture and acknowledge that there is more to your life than meets the eye. When you're paying attention to synchronicity, you're listening to the messages of a benevolent universe that gently guides you on your path.

On your journey, you'll discover that synchronicities come in many guises. They can be as simple as thinking an uncommon word or phrase, then hearing it moments later on television or the radio. Or they can be so complex and layered that you must make connections and associations to interpret them.

A synchronicity can serve not only as guidance, but also as a warning, an affirmation, creative inspiration, or evidence of psychological growth. It can offer a glimpse into your future, and cause you to feel you're on the right track, in the groove, exactly where you're supposed to be. By their very nature, synchronicities are mysterious, yet pertinent.

Awareness of synchronicity is key. By recording your synchronicities as they occur, you increase your awareness. When your awareness is heightened, you experience more synchros. It's like an inviolate mathematical axiom. Your synchro journal will provide a track record of your journey and over time will reveal secrets that you couldn't comprehend at the time of the events.

Now get ready. Your first synchronicity after reading this introduction could happen at any moment, just as it did for us along that highway. After all, you're expecting the miraculous, right? You might walk out to your car, turn on the radio and hear someone say the word *synchronicity*. Or you might bump into a friend you were thinking about earlier, someone you hadn't seen in weeks, months, maybe years. Maybe he or she says, "What a coincidence. I've got something that belongs to you in my car. It's an old album by The Police. You know the one, *Synchronicity.*"

THE KNOWING

Once we recognize coincidence as meaningful, we open ourselves to new information, new possibilities, new belief systems.

A Question for You. State the question you'd most like answered about your life. Keep it simple and specific. Think about your question periodically as you write in this journal. By the time you've filled its pages, you'll have an answer, by using your intuition.

_____

_____

_____

_____

_____

_____

_____

_____

_____

_____

_____

_____

_____

_____

_____

_____

_____

_____

Developing Awareness. The best way to develop awareness of synchronicities—and, therefore, to experience more of them—is to keep track of them. Describe a seemingly coincidental event in as much detail as possible. Make sure you not only note the time, date, and place where the synchronicity occurred, but also describe how you felt at the time it was happening. Can you link it to events taking place in your life? What symbols were involved?

_____

_____

_____

_____

_____

_____

_____

_____

_____

_____

_____

_____

_____

_____

_____

_____

_____

_____

_____

_____

_____

_____

_____

_____

_____

_____

_____

_____

_____

_____

_____

_____

_____

_____

_____

_____

_____

_____

_____

_____

_____

_____

Symbols. A *symbol* is an object, image, situation, or event that represents something else. Its full meaning may be blatantly obvious, or it may elude us or lie altogether beyond our comprehension. A symbol might appear to you as a peculiar cloud pattern, the unexpected sighting of an animal, the discovery of an unusual object, a hidden message delivered in a casual conversation. They hold messages and clues about the patterns in our lives. By becoming aware of them and understanding their significance, we gradually learn the language of symbols and are able to unlock the messages of such synchronicities more easily. Have you encountered a symbol recently? If so, what was it? Did you recognize it as a symbol initially? If not, what changed your mind? How was the symbol significant to what was occurring to your life at the time?

_____

_____

_____

_____

_____

_____

_____

_____

_____

_____

Taking Stock. Think of a meaningful coincidence, a sign, or an omen you experienced. What was going on in your life at the time? Were huge odds involved? Was it something you talked about with family and friends? Who else was involved? Did your meaningful coincidence, sign, or omen strike you as confirmation? A warning? Did it seem to be urging you to move in a new direction?

_____

_____

_____

_____

_____

_____

_____

_____

_____

_____

_____

_____

_____

_____

_____

_____

_____

_____

Finding Meaning in Coincidental Events. Think back to a seemingly coincidental event and consider how the synchronicity might be meaningful. Does it affirm something you're feeling, doing, or contemplating? Does it transmit a message? Does it awaken you to a new path? Over time, you may discover that many of your synchronicities are centered around particular themes—emotional highs and lows, creativity, your career, travel, family or friends, animals and pets. Once you recognize how and when synchronicities are most likely to occur for you, it's easier to attract them.

_____

_____

_____

_____

_____

_____

_____

_____

_____

_____

_____

_____

_____

_____

_____

_____

_____

_____
_____
_____
_____
_____
_____
_____
_____
_____
_____
_____
_____
_____
_____
_____
_____
_____
_____
_____
_____
_____
_____
_____
_____
_____
_____
_____

Recognizing Coincidences. Every time you experience a coincidence, consider the possibility that it might be meaningful. If you overlook or simply shrug off coincidences as insignificant, you miss opportunities to gain new understanding or a fresh look at some aspect of your life. For example, have you ever felt discouraged about a relationship, your job, your finances, and you're about to give up? Then something unexpected occurs that makes you realize things aren't as dire as you thought. How did you react? Did you dismiss the incident as an interesting but random coincidence? Did you act on it?

Harnessing Synchronicity. Everything you see in your personal life—family, home, loved ones, pets, children and partners, career triumphs and losses, your health and prosperity—is a result of intentions and beliefs you hold, desires you have. Think of a question. Or, focus on a goal. Make it something meaningful. What do you really want or really need? When the question or goal comes to you, make it specific, yet simple. Write it down, tell your friends. Put the word out to the universe.

Look for something unusual in your environment, something unexpected. Maybe it's a call from someone you haven't talked to for a long time. Or a chance meeting with someone. Any unexpected encounter could provide a forum for obtaining your answer. What's the first thing the person says to you? Can you find a meaning related to your question or goal? Does it offer you direction, a new approach, or maybe a warning? If you're not certain, watch for the next synchronicity while you keep thinking about your question or goal.

_____

_____

_____

_____

_____

_____

_____

_____

Expressing Gratitude. You may want to do what author, publisher, and medical intuitive Louise Hay does every morning. Before she even gets out of bed, she expresses her gratitude for everything in her life. It's a beautiful habit to cultivate. And the universe will always respond by bringing more experiences, situations, and people into your life to appreciate. Take a moment to jot down people, situations, and things you are grateful for and why.

_____

_____

_____

_____

_____

_____

_____

_____

_____

_____

_____

_____

_____

_____

_____

_____

THE HEART

Synchronicities are deeply intertwined with our emotions.

Pay Attention to Your Feelings. When you experience a synchronicity, write down all the details involved in the experience and also pay special attention to your emotional state. Were you happy, feeling low, or somewhere in between? Why do you think you were feeling that way? Your emotions are an accurate barometer of what is right, wrong, or unsettled in your life.

_____

_____

_____

_____

_____

_____

_____

_____

_____

_____

_____

_____

_____

_____

_____

_____

_____

_____

Making Lists. When you feel out of sorts, list the thing in your life that you would most like to change. Remember, you can't change other people, but you can change yourself. Next, list the things you love about your life. Once, you elevate your mood, chances are a synchronicity will manifest that not only reflects your improved mood, but also offers guidance, insight, and hope.

_____

_____

_____

_____

_____

_____

_____

_____

_____

_____

_____

_____

_____

_____

_____

_____

_____

_____

_____

Connections to People. Our relationships provide richly textured atmospheres for the occurrence of synchronicity. Friendships connect us to something larger than ourselves, awakening us to a mysterious realm that exists outside of cause and effect. Take a few minutes to think about the people outside of your own family who have played important roles in your life. How did you meet? Why did your friendships develop? Look for anything extraordinary or mysterious in the original encounters.

_____

_____

_____

_____

_____

_____

_____

_____

_____

_____

_____

_____

_____

_____

_____

_____

_____

_____

_____

_____

_____

_____

_____

_____

_____

_____

_____

_____

_____

_____

_____

_____

_____

_____

_____

_____

_____

_____

_____

_____

Connections to Places. At some time in your life you may feel strongly connected to a particular place. These connections are intensely emotional, archetypal, and often psychic in that they speak to some deeper level. Perhaps it's a connection that seems to complete you in some way, or makes a statement about who you really are or wish to become. Describe in detail a place that you feel connected to. How are you connected to it? Is it a vacation destination that you visit over and over or perhaps a place you dream of living in? Sometimes this connection is so emotionally charged it draws a particular experience your way through the law of attraction and awakens you to some greater potential.

Distinguishing Between Chance and Meaningful Coincidences.
We experience synchronicities for reasons that may not be immediately obvious, and when they manifest themselves through
impulses, we need to act, to follow the impulse. Think of an emotional time in your own life when your inner world seemed to
coincide with an outer event. Did you dismiss the experience as
random and without meaning? Or did you recognize the experience as significant? Were you able to use the synchronicity to make
a decision?

_____

_____

_____

_____

_____

_____

_____

_____

_____

_____

_____

_____

_____

_____

Where Do You Place Your Attention? Anything in your environment can hint at synchronicity. In the course of a given day, notice where you place your attention. Is there a particular corner or neighborhood that you pass on the way to work that always seems to reach out to you? How does it make you feel? Why does it attract you? It may be that you're tuning in emotionally to a synchronicity that lies ahead.

_____

_____

_____

_____

_____

_____

_____

_____

_____

_____

_____

_____

_____

_____

_____

_____

_____

_____

_____

_____

_____

_____

_____

_____

_____

_____

_____

_____

_____

_____

_____

_____

_____

_____

_____

_____

_____

_____

_____

_____

_____

_____

_____

_____

Emotional Impact. When we bring our intentions and desires into the equation, magic happens. There are times when we want something so badly and are willing to do the work necessary to bring about change that the universe responds quickly, literally, in a way we can't dismiss as random coincidence. Think back to a time when you worked really hard to obtain a desired goal. Describe the situation. Did you get what you wanted? If so, did it come quickly? Were you surprised by the coincidence? How did it make you feel?

_____

_____

_____

_____

_____

_____

_____

_____

_____

_____

_____

_____

_____

_____

_____

_____

Sensing the Future. Emotions often play a role in synchronicities, including incidents of precognition. Think about an important relationship outside of your immediate family, especially a love interest. Try to remember the first time you met. Describe what thoughts you had and how you felt. Did you feel an immediate connection, sense that a close, long-term relationship would develop? Continue to pay close attention to your thoughts and feelings as important events unfold in your life. Try to guess what will come about, based on your intuitive thoughts and feelings. Later, look back and see how well you did.

_____

_____

_____

_____

_____

_____

_____

_____

_____

_____

_____

_____

_____

_____

THE THEORY

Synchronicity is the granddaddy of all paranormal phenomena, telepathy, precognition, clairvoyance, and remote viewing.

Psychic Phenomena. Forget whatever you think you know about psychic phenomena. Instead, recall the last time you had a hunch about something, a gut feeling, and acted on it. Or, think about the dream you had that later came true. Describe your dream, feeling, or impulse in detail. What happened later on that confirmed that your experience was a psychic phenomena? How did this make you feel? When you experience something like this, you're already familiar with synchronicity, which lies at the heart of all things psychic.

_____

_____

_____

_____

_____

_____

_____

_____

_____

_____

_____

_____

_____

_____

_____

_____

The Power of Touch. There is a strong relationship between emotions and synchronicity. Someone who is "empathic" tunes into the emotions and physical sensations of the person or object they are trying to read. Known as psychometry or psychic touch, this ability enables them to read the thoughts that impregnate objects.

You might've experienced psychic touch yourself when picking up an old object or visiting an ancient site. Have you ever sensed someone staring at you, or felt someone's presence in a room before you knew anyone was there? Do you get strong feelings, or a flood of emotions and memories, when you look at old photographs? Have you ever entered a room and sensed that an argument or other emotionally charged event had just taken place? Do you sense other people's moods and adapt to them as if they were your own? Think back to one of these moments and write down what you felt. What impressions did you get? Did you find out if they were true?

_____

_____

_____

_____

_____

_____

_____

_____

_____

_____

_____

_____

_____

_____

_____

_____

_____

_____

_____

_____

_____

_____

_____

_____

_____

_____

_____

_____

_____

_____

_____

_____

_____

Remote Viewing Exercise. *Clairvoyance*, or remote viewing, is a psychic skill that falls within the realm of synchronicity. It's an extrasensory talent that allows you to see something beyond the range of your normal vision.

Even if you've never had a spontaneous clairvoyant experience, you can learn techniques to help you glimpse scenes taking place elsewhere. Have a friend go into another room and choose a small object, then place it in a bag, box, or envelope so that you cannot possibly know what it is. The best objects are those with sensory details.

Your mission is to identify the object, using your psychic power. Close your eyes and begin to write down your impressions. If you prefer, draw the object.

Now ask your friend to bring you the object he selected. Hold it in your hands. Feel it and sense all its qualities. Note which characteristics came through to you clearly and which ones were faint or missed altogether. Did you get sidetracked by the tendency to over-analyze? Learn to distinguish between the mind's idle chatter and psychic functioning. Remote viewing usually manifests as subtle, fleeting messages or images that come to mind when you quiet the chatter.

_____

_____

_____

_____

THE CREATIVE

Creativity lies at the heart of synchronicity.

Creativity, Rituals, and Synchronicity. We all have the ability to create new possibilities through our imaginations and intent; ritual is one way of focusing that intent. At every level of creativity—from conception to execution—rituals play a vital role. What kind of rituals do you use in your creative work? Do you have a technique for summoning your muse? Is there a certain time of the day or night when you're most creative? The kinds of rituals you use are unique to you and the type of creative work you do. Once you get into the habit, synchronicity won't be far behind.

_____

_____

_____

_____

_____

_____

_____

_____

_____

_____

_____

_____

_____

_____

_____

How Open Are You? New experiences are the foundation of any creative process. They help us to see the world and ourselves in new ways. They stimulate new ideas and open us to new possibilities. So before you dive into your creative passion, determine how open you are to new experiences. How often do you embrace new experiences? Describe a recent new experience in detail. Did you take a risk? Were you seeking excitement? How did the experience make you feel?

_____

_____

_____

_____

_____

_____

_____

_____

_____

_____

_____

_____

_____

_____

_____

Positive Affirmations and Creativity. Most of us have a creative talent or interest we would like to nurture and develop. However, if you never take the leap of faith and believe in yourself, you'll never know just how creative you are. Jot down statements that will inspire creativity and drive like "Whatever I can imagine, I can manifest," and "Whatever I need comes to me." These statements are affirmations that help pave the way for your creative self-expression. Mull them over. Make them true. The more you practice such positive affirmations, the more you invite synchronicity into your life, which in turn helps to guide you on your creative path. Nurturing your creativity and opening yourself up allows for synchronicities that could lead you to the right opportunities and people at the right time.

_____

_____

_____

_____

_____

_____

_____

_____

_____

_____

_____

_____

_____

_____

_____

_____

_____

_____

_____

_____

_____

_____

_____

_____

_____

_____

_____

_____

Manifestation as a Creative Art. As with any other creative endeavor, the more you practice manifestation, the better you become at it. The greater your proficiency, the greater the possibility that synchronicity will coincide with your manifestations. In fact, they may be one and the same.

Think of three objects you would like to see or find today, objects you know will make you feel joyful. Spend a few moments concentrating on these objects. See each object vividly in your imagination, holding the image in your mind for at least a minute and a half. Fully describe your objects in your journal and then go about your day. If you've visualized vividly, then it's likely you will find each of these objects within a matter of hours, but not necessarily in the way you expect. For example, say one of your objects is a dragonfly; you may push your shopping cart across the supermarket parking lot and notice a dragonfly hovering above the shrubbery in the median. At the end of the day, think back and describe how each object appeared to you. What did their appearance signify for you?

_____

_____

_____

_____

_____

_____

_____

_____

Engaging Your Creativity. Try devising a written plan outlining everything you want to achieve in your creative life for the week, month, year. Update it as needed and keep revising. Look at it frequently. Read it or recite it from heart, and back it with passion.

Fueling Your Creativity. All of us are inherently creative, therefore what we *do* is less important than what we think and feel about what we're doing in any given moment.

When you're looking for an innovative solution or a new way of doing something—at home, in your work, with your children—where do you start? Do you fret and rage, complain and worry? Do you feel anxious? These emotions will only attract more of the same. Instead of railing at the universe because you can't find a solution or feel blocked, take a deep breath. Then send a clear signal to the universe that you want to experience synchronicities related to your concerns.

Unlocking Your Creativity. Sometimes when you're involved in a creative project, you encounter blocks. Your best efforts to move ahead get stymied. Once you accept that occasional blocks are normal, you can use synchronicity to overcome difficulties. Here's one idea: move away from your workplace and listen to what other people are saying, whether they are talking to you or to each other. Or, maybe you hear someone talking on the radio or television. Catch a few phrases and jot them down. Even if what you hear has nothing to do with your project, give it a chance. Play with the words. Look for hidden hints. How can they apply to your problem?

_____

_____

_____

_____

_____

_____

_____

_____

_____

_____

_____

_____

_____

_____

Creativity and Dreams. As you're falling asleep, do so with the intention that you will recall any and all dreams that are relevant to what you're working on or are concerned about. When you wake up after a relevant dream, jot down any details you remember. As you become proficient at remembering your last dream of the night, you will learn how to work your way back through each successive dream so that you may be able to recall four or five dreams. Over time, the lexicon of your dream world will emerge and you'll be able to interpret your dreams with greater ease.

_____

_____

_____

_____

_____

_____

_____

_____

_____

_____

_____

_____

_____

_____

Creating the Future. Sometimes you may not realize the relationship between a synchronicity and the creative process until long after the creative effort is complete. Since everything in the universe is intimately connected, you can compose a short story linked to a future event. Tell yourself that the creative part of you is not tied to the present but can travel into the future. Jot down details and impressions that come to mind. Don't worry about writing style or punctuation. Once you've finished, keep your eyes open for an event that resembles your story.

_____

_____

_____

_____

_____

_____

_____

_____

_____

_____

_____

_____

_____

_____

_____

THE CLUSTERS

Synchronicity manifests itself in clusters of numbers, names, objects, words, symbols.

Interpreting Clusters. Clusters of numbers, names, words, phrases, songs, objects, and events are one of the most curious aspects of synchronicity. The meanings of such clusters may not be immediately apparent when you experience them. But by interpreting them as metaphors, by doing some research and using your intuition, you can gain clarity and a deeper appreciation for how your inner self, your unconscious, guides you. Select a question regarding an issue or concern that's important to you. Then request that some sort of cluster appear during the day, that you'll be able to relate it to your question. Jot down events that happen throughout the day. Over time, a pattern should emerge.

_____

_____

_____

_____

_____

_____

_____

_____

_____

_____

_____

_____

_____

_____

_____

_____

_____

_____

_____

_____

_____

_____

_____

_____

_____

_____

_____

_____

_____

_____

_____

_____

_____

_____

_____

_____

_____

_____

Your Number Clusters. Number clusters often attract attention and can be referred to as "stalkers," wake-up calls, or as integral to a spiritual journey. Whenever you experience a synchronicity of number clusters, such as 11, 111, and 11:11 or 3, 33, jot down what was happening at the time. Note your mood, emotions, who was with you, all the circumstantial details. Over time, a pattern should emerge. You may discover the clusters tend to appear at certain periods of the day—at night, for instance, or when you're driving or in a relaxed state.

Understanding Your Number Cluster. Sometimes, the appearance of a cluster of numbers encourages awareness, awakening you to the mysteries of the universe. Think back to an experience with number clusters. For instance, say that in the space of several hours, you experience a cluster of 8s. Your grocery store bill was $88.08, your lunch cost exactly $8.88, and you received your mortgage bill for $888.88. To decipher the message, begin with what the number 8 means to you. Is it your lucky number? With what do you associate it? Have you experienced sequences of 8 before? If so, what were the circumstances? If nothing comes to mind, research the number. Study its esoteric symbolism and see if something resonates.

We all have the ability to
create new possibilities through
our imaginations and intent
ritual is one way of focusing
that intent.

Other Types of Clusters. Some people never experience synchronicities involving number clusters. But they experience clusters of names, phrases, places, even dates. Synchronistic clusters involving names, phrases, places, and/or dates may be addressing a future event, situation, or relationship, a situation occurring now, a deeper issue, or another event you may be unaware of. Research the clusters' etymology. There could be a message in the root of the word or name. Note the source. A dream? Images on TV or in magazines? How often are they repeated—within minutes, days, weeks? Do they disappear for a while, then start again? Watch for patterns. Correlate the cluster patterns to events occurring in your life or in the lives of people to whom you're close. The point is to identify clusters, find meaning, insight, and information, and see how you can utilize it.

_____

_____

_____

_____

_____

_____

_____

_____

_____

_____

THE TRICKSTER

A synchronicity can reveal itself with a twist of humor or wry irony so startling it stops us in our tracks.

Understanding Your Trickster. Trickster synchronicities inspire awe, astonishment, even shock. They can prompt you to re-evaluate relationships, consider alternative career paths, and make choices you might not have considered otherwise. Nearly always, you initially feel as if you're the brunt of the universe's joke. The trick with the trickster is to dig beneath the joke to discover what's really going on. Write down one of your trickster experiences. Why do you think you've attracted this particular experience? Look for metaphors, make associations, request a dream that will shed light on the issue. Have you told others about your trickster, and if so, what have they said? If you let other people in on your trickster stories, they might come up with possible meanings that never would occur to you.

_____

_____

_____

_____

_____

_____

_____

_____

_____

_____

_____

_____

Working with the Trickster Element. Synchronicities are sometimes found in your immediate environment through the behavior of birds and other animals, weather patterns, a voice on the radio or TV. You can attempt to generate synchronicities and even specific types, such as trickster synchronicities. Tell yourself you're going to experience synchronicity, perhaps one of the trickster variety—but be sure to add that the experience will not harm you or anyone else. Stay alert for "coincidental" encounters that might otherwise slip by you unnoticed. At the end of the day, record significant experiences in detail. Did an event jolt you into a higher awareness of the interconnection between the mundane and the extraordinary? If so, what do you think was the meaning behind this trickster?

_____

_____

_____

_____

_____

_____

_____

_____

_____

_____

_____

THE GLOBAL

When synchronicities manifest themselves
through global events, the universe seems to be
addressing us as a collective.

Nationally Observed Synchronicities. Through mass events and the synchronicities so often associated with them, the universe speaks to us as a collective—as a people, a community, a nation, as citizens of the same planet. These types of synchronicities certainly illustrate connections to a deeper layer of existence. Take a few moments to think about mass events—disasters, invasions, large-scale demonstrations, deaths of public figures—and try to remember any synchronicities related to them. Did you have a dream or premonition about such an event? Did you have a connection with someone involved in the event, or a connection with the location? Chances are that the events, which captured your attention, carried some personal significance.

_____

_____

_____

_____

_____

_____

_____

_____

_____

_____

_____

_____

Thinking Globally. What, exactly, is this global mind? It's the combined consciousness of every person on the planet. The global mind—the *unus mundus*—is where the source of meaningful coincidence is separate from our conscious awareness and egos, but it's where the psyche and the external world touch. With eyes closed, lay your hand on a newspaper. Once you feel centered, take away your hand and stare "through" the newspaper. Allow your vision to "unfocus." When images of headlines appear, jot them down. A day or two later, look in the newspaper and see if those exact or similar headlines appear. When we allow ourselves to look, to *really* look, our rational minds reel about future events.

_____

_____

_____

_____

_____

_____

_____

_____

_____

_____

_____

_____

_____

Synchronicities and Global Events. Because we share the planet with nearly seven billion people, it behooves us to pay attention to what's going on in the larger world and to look for synchronicities related to global events that may hold vital clues about future trends. Think about your most recent global synchronicities and arrange them by categories, such as politics, international affairs, famous people, finances/economy, disasters, and war. In which category do you notice the most synchronicities? What kinds of synchronicities do you find? Metaphorical? Precognitive? Literal? Why do you think you have more of one kind than another?

_____

_____

_____

_____

_____

_____

_____

_____

_____

_____

_____

_____

_____

_____

DIVINING
SYNCHRONICITY

Divination is the most tangible way to engage synchronicity.

Quick and Easy Divination. Write down your question, and simply tell yourself that the next thing you hear, see, or read will provide an answer. Maybe the answer lies in the headline of the morning paper, or something said on television. Make sure you write down any information that relates to your question. How does the information fit your question? If you can't find any connection, drop it and look for the next possibility. If that doesn't work, it could indicate you're not meant to receive an answer now. It also could suggest you don't want to accept the answer that was presented to you. Wait an hour or a day, then try again. One way or another, you *will* get your answer.

Daily Tarot Diary. Draw a tarot card to get a sense of your day. Allow the image to speak to the deeper part of you and write your impressions down here. When you're finished, compare what you've written to the meanings in a tarot book.

_____

_____

_____

_____

_____

_____

_____

_____

_____

_____

_____

_____

_____

_____

_____

_____

_____

_____

_____

_____

_____

Using Astrology. Astrology is a divination tool that considers the patterns and movements of the heavenly bodies at any given time. It uses a natal chart or horoscope, which is determined by the date, time, and place of your birth. If you don't know the degree of your natal sun, go to *www.astro.com* for a free copy of your natal chart. Locate the sun—its symbol looks like a circle with a dot in the center. Next to it you will find numbers that indicate the degree of the sign in which your natal sun is placed. If you were born on October 14, for example, your sun would be in 20 degrees of Libra. This means there may have been a defining moment in your life when you were around twenty years old. Give it six months or so on either side. If you have reached that age, describe your defining moment. What happened and how did it make you feel? When did you have the experience? If you're not yet at the age that corresponds with the degree of your natal sun, keep in mind that some defining event may happen when you reach that age, and make sure to record the happenings.

_____

_____

_____

_____

_____

_____

_____

_____

***The* I Ching.** *I Ching* has been around for thousands of years. It
is a divination system based on sixty-four patterns known as hexa-
grams, which are derived by tossing three coins six times. Head
to your nearest bookstore and look for one of the many editions
about *I Ching*. Our favorite is the popular Richard Wilhelm/Cary
F. Baynes edition. Take your translation into the café, order a cof-
fee, get out three pennies, and think of a question. Then toss your
coins and see what happens. Write down your interpretation. How
does it relate to events in your life? What does it mean to you?
When you're able to relate an interpretation to events in your life,
you gain guidance from the unconscious mind, which is linked
to the underlying reality, the collective unconscious. In essence,
the practice of divination is our most immediate contact with
synchronicity.

_____

_____

_____

_____

_____

_____

_____

_____

_____

_____

Stichomancy. This divination system is quick and easy—and amazingly accurate. Think of a question or issue that concerns you. Hold it in your mind, open any book (a dictionary, the *Bible* or other religious text, *Grimm's Fairy Tales*, your favorite novel or nonfiction book, even a magazine) at random, and point to a place on the page. Does the word, phrase, or picture your finger touched illuminate your question or concern? Consider the symbology of the source you used. Does what you pointed to reveal a deeper meaning given the source? For additional insight, take note of the particular section of the source. If you get an ambiguous answer, try again and phrase your question differently. Or, when you point at a word, read the entire sentence or paragraph.

ANIMAL ORACLES

"Everyone has been touched by animals in some way, either in life or in dreams, and always the difficulty is determining what it means."

—TED ANDREWS, *ANIMAL-WISE*

Animals as Symbols. Animals are among the most accessible synchronistic symbols available to you. When an animal appears to you—especially one you wouldn't normally see in the course of your ordinary day, or that shows up under unusual circumstances—write down what you were thinking about or doing at the time. Research the animal's meaning. How does its meaning relate to your feelings or actions? The sighting could be a verification that you're making the right decision. However, the animal's appearance, or its actions, could warn you that you're about to make a bad decision.

Animals as Messengers. Different animals may appear synchronistically at different times, for specific reasons. The reason may not always be apparent to you at the time, but you'll intuitively feel the connection. Consider a question or matter that concerns you, then during the day, watch for the appearance of an animal. When you experience an animal synchronicity—either in real life or in a dream—write down your own impressions and interpretations. When you're finished, research the animal for possible clues to its message.

_____

_____

_____

_____

_____

_____

_____

_____

_____

_____

_____

_____

_____

_____

_____

Your Own Animal Glossary. Many of the animal meanings within books will fit your experiences. It's likely, however, that you'll also discover many of your own animal sightings mean different things to you. If you're terrified of dogs, for example, you probably won't associate them with unconditional love and acceptance. For you, it may be an omen that something frightening is coming into your life. Create your own animal glossary to keep track of your animal experiences. Make sure you not only include the animal and insights regarding the animal, but also the synchronicities that unfold and any other detail that seems significant.

JOURNEYS

"Beyond the obvious increased opportunities it provides for encountering meaningful coincidences, travel is itself a transformational experience."

—FRANK JOSEPH, *SYNCHRONICITY & YOU*

Travel Experiences. Whether you're headed across town or across the world, travel removes you from normal routines and habitual thinking. You're exposed to new experiences, uncanny encounters, and all the high strangeness the universe can muster. Start your day expecting synchronicity. After all, when you're on a journey, unexpected things happen. At the end of the day, jot down your thoughts about the day's events. Did anything strange occur? Did your plans change throughout the day? Look for synchronicities and how unexpected incidents changed your path.

Dreaming of the Future. Before going to bed, suggest to yourself that you'll have a dream of an upcoming event. Upon awakening, jot down any dream images you remember. Don't try to interpret them, but note as many details as possible. Later on in the month, review your dreams to see if any of the scenarios actually hinted at future events and elaborate on how the scenarios are similar.

_____

_____

_____

_____

_____

_____

_____

_____

_____

_____

_____

_____

_____

_____

_____

_____

_____

_____

Messages from the Afterlife. Mystics have always said we take regular nighttime journeys into reams of the afterlife that we don't remember when we wake up. Yet, dreams of contact with loved ones from the afterlife are striking. You might feel a surge of energy, as if you're more alive than usual.

You may experience such a dream near the time a relative or someone close to you dies. The contact might occur spontaneously without any effort on your part.

When you wake up, ask yourself what you dreamed. Sometimes just the effort triggers your memory. Who did you come in contact with during your dream? Did you and your loved one have a conversation? If so, what was it about? Did he or she say anything significant to current events in your life? How did you feel during this experience? Try to jot down as many details as you can. Often, our loved one's message is clear and inspiring.

Reaching Out. You can also ask to contact someone in a dream. Let's say you want to contact your grandfather, who died recently. You were close to him and have many fond memories of your times together.

Write down a happy time you spent together with your grandfather. How did it make you feel? Recall as many details as possible. As you settle into bed, relax and take a few deep breaths. Tell yourself you're about to launch a journey to make contact with your grandfather and think about the moment you wrote down. Sink deeper into a meditative state as you picture yourself with your grandfather. In your drowsy state, you imagine hearing a response. See if you can continue the conversation. When you wake up, write down the conversation you had with your loved one. If you didn't make contact, you might encounter one or more synchronicities during the day that are directly related to memories of your loved one.

_____

_____

_____

_____

_____

_____

_____

_____

_____

BEYOND HERE

Sure, this world is fascinating, but *what's beyond is even more intriguing...*

Want a place to share stories and experiences about all things strange and unusual? From UFOs and apparitions to dream interpretation, the Tarot, astrology, and more, the **BEYOND HERE** blog is the newest hot spot for paranormal activity!

Sign up for our newsletter at
www.adamsmedia.com/blog/paranormal
and download our free Haunted U.S. Hot Spots Map!